# BENEDICT XVI

# *Spiritual Thoughts*

## IN THE FIRST YEAR OF HIS PAPACY

UNITED STATES CONFERENCE OF CATHOLIC BISHOPS
WASHINGTON, D.C.

First printing, March 2007

Printed in Canada
ISBN-10: 1-57455-765-3
ISBN-13: 978-1-57455-765-7
USCCB Publishing
3211 Fourth Street, NE
Washington, DC 20017-1194
www.usccbpublishing.org

FSC

**Mixed Sources**
Product group from well-managed
forests and other controlled sources

Cert no. SW-COC-789
www.fsc.org
© 1996 Forest Stewardship Council

# CONTENTS

# PREFACE

He who does not give God gives too little.
— BENEDICT XVI

These *Spiritual Thoughts* of Pope Benedict XVI have been gathered from the first year of his pontificate. They have been chosen from an extensive selection of texts including homilies, catecheses, audiences, the *angelus*, messages, and speeches delivered during meetings, trips, and interviews, as well as the occasional impromptu observation.

To several of these passages, already of major theological significance, is added a formidable spiritual dimension: able to reach, directly and immediately, the heart and soul of the reader and the listener on topics that are crucial to the human experience. The words and the thoughts of Pope Benedict often have a tone and feeling that, by the images evoked, achieve the strength and the clarity of true poetic fragments. They awaken in each one of us a fresh perspective from which we can reflect on our faith, look to the Scriptures, observe our present difficulties, and in general bring ourselves closer to what is essential, through the model of Jesus' simplicity and richness – as Pope Benedict said in a speech to the clergy of the Diocese of Aoste (July 25, 2005): "Faith is simple and rich: we believe that God exists, that God counts; but which God? A God with a face, a human face, a God who reconciles, who overcomes hatred and gives us the power of peace that no one else can give us."

While contemplating the 175 thoughts that constitute this collection, the reader will notice that the most frequent themes focus on faith in God, the centrality of Jesus, and the love that is given to us, that we must transform into the gift of self. Yet these thoughts always express an awareness of the social and cultural reality that constitutes the horizon of the world of this 21st century, with all its limitations – secularism, relativism, materialism, individualism, hedonism – that stem from our losing sight of our relationship of "friendship" with Jesus, a relationship that helps us to distinguish between good and evil, truth and falsehood. Without this relationship we are lost. We lose sight of a sense of certainty, of truth, and of our responsibility in the world.

Suffering, holiness, faith education of adults and especially of young people, life, family, peace, freedom, happiness – all have become the focus of Pope Benedict's other "thoughts" in this book. And the frequency with which these themes occur demonstrates his undeniable interest and real concern for these subjects and the problems facing humanity today. Each and every time he reflects on these challenges, he never tires of encouraging and recalling this fundamental moment in human existence: the meeting with the Person of Christ, an encounter "which gives life a new horizon" (*Deus caritas est*, no. 1) – a meeting able to transform and open up our own true and authentic person, able to enlighten our lives, "to make the truth."

This anthology offers only a glimpse of the teachings of Pope Benedict XVI. These brief passages cannot even remotely claim to reflect a proper image of the complexity and depth of his teachings. These excerpts are offered to readers in the way they were presented to me when I first read and listened to what the Holy Father wrote and said.

The spiritual richness of this experience is precisely what I wished to convey while selecting and ordering the passages. I now make them available for meditative and personal reading, so that these insights, these nuances, these teachings may not be lost in the ebb and flow of events and time.

Lucio Coco

NOTE
The documents from which this anthology was drawn can be found in full on the Web site of the Apostolic See in the section concerning Pope Benedict XVI: *www. vatican.va/holy_father/benedict_xvi/index.htm.*

The sources for thoughts 26, 27, and 28 can be found on the official site of the Vatican Radio in the section relating to the Holy Father: *www.oecumene.radiovaticana.org/ en1/benedict_XVI_itv.asp.*

BENEDICT XVI

*Spiritual Thoughts*

[MARCH 2005 - APRIL 2006]

## APRIL 2005

### 1. The foundation

At this point, my mind goes back to October 22, 1978, when Pope John Paul II began his ministry here in St. Peter's Square. His words on that occasion constantly echo in my ears: "Do not be afraid! Open wide the doors for Christ!" The Pope was addressing the mighty, the powerful of this world, who feared that Christ might take away something of their power if they were to let him in, if they were to allow the faith to be free. Yes, he would certainly have taken something away from them: the dominion of corruption, the manipulation of law, and the freedom to do as they pleased. But he would not have taken away anything that pertains to human freedom or dignity, or to the building of a just society.

*Homily at the inaugural Pontifical Mass*
*in St. Peter's Square*
*April 24, 2005*

## 2. Spiritual deserts

And there are so many kinds of desert. There is the desert of poverty, the desert of hunger and thirst, the desert of abandonment, of loneliness, of destroyed love. There is the desert of God's darkness, the emptiness of souls no longer aware of their dignity or the goal of human life. The external deserts in the world are growing, because the internal deserts have become so vast.

*Homily at the inaugural Pontifical Mass*
*in St. Peter's Square*
*April 24, 2005*

## 3. Patience

God, who became a lamb, tells us that the world is saved by the Crucified One, not by those who crucified him. The world is redeemed by the patience of God. It is destroyed by the impatience of man.

*Homily at the inaugural Pontifical Mass*
*in St. Peter's Square*
*April 24, 2005*

## 4. In friendship with Christ

If we let Christ into our lives, we lose nothing, nothing, absolutely nothing of what makes life free, beautiful, and great. No! Only in this friendship are the doors of life opened wide. Only in this friendship is the great potential of human existence truly revealed. Only in this friendship do we experience beauty and liberation.

*Homily at the inaugural Pontifical Mass*
*in St. Peter's Square, April 24, 2005*

## 5. Christ is central

We are familiar with the recommendation that this father of western monasticism [St. Benedict] left to his monks in his Rule: "Prefer nothing to the love of Christ" (Rule 72:11; cf. 4:21). At the beginning of my service as Successor of Peter, I ask St. Benedict to help us keep Christ firmly at the heart of our lives. May Christ always have pride of place in our thoughts and in all our activities!

*Catechesis to the General Audience, April 27, 2005*

## MAY 2005

### 6. Close to us

Each one of us can be on intimate terms with him; each can call upon him. The Lord is always within hearing. We can inwardly draw away from him. We can live turning our backs on him. But he always waits for us and is always close to us.

*Homily at the Mass of Possession of the Chair of*
*the Bishop of Rome in the Basilica of St. John Lateran*
*May 7, 2005*

### 7. Scripture and its interpreters

Whenever Sacred Scripture is separated from the living voice of the Church, it falls prey to disputes among experts. Of course, all they have to tell us is important and invaluable; the work of scholars is a considerable help in understanding the living process in which the Scriptures developed, hence, also in grasping their historical richness. Yet science alone cannot provide us with a definitive and binding interpretation; it is unable to offer us, in its interpretation, that certainty with which we can live and for which we can even die.

*Homily at the Mass of Possession of the Chair of*
*the Bishop of Rome in the Basilica of St. John Lateran*
*May 7, 2005*

## 8. Fear and fright

This attitude of faith leads men and women to recognize the power of God who works in history and thus to open themselves to feeling awe for the name of the Lord. In biblical language, in fact, this "fear" is not fright, it does not denote fear, for fear of God is something quite different. It is recognition of the mystery of divine transcendence.

*Catechesis to the General Audience*
*May 11, 2005*

## 9. The priesthood

In fact, all that constitutes our priestly ministry cannot be the product of our personal abilities. This is true for the administration of the Sacraments, but it is also true for the service of the Word: we are not sent to proclaim ourselves or our personal opinions, but the mystery of Christ and, in him, the measure of true humanism.

*Address to the clergy of Rome in*
*the Basilica of St. John Lateran*
*May 13, 2005*

## 10. Communion and the Church

The Christian faith is not something purely spiritual and internal, nor is our relationship with Christ itself exclusively subjective and private. Rather, it is a completely concrete and ecclesial relationship.

*Address to the clergy of Rome in*
*the Basilica of St. John Lateran*
*May 13, 2005*

## 11. A plural freedom

Human freedom is always a shared freedom, a "togetherness" of liberty. Common freedom lasts only in an ordered harmony of freedom that reveals to each person his or her limits.

*Homily for Pentecost at St. Peter's Basilica*
*May 15, 2005*

## 12. Closing of hearts

The Risen Lord passes through the closed doors and enters the place where the disciples are, and greets them twice with the words: "Peace be with you." We continually close our doors; we continually want to feel secure and do not want to be disturbed by others and by God. And so, we can continually implore the Lord just for this, that he come to us, overcoming our closure, to bring us his greeting: "Peace be with you." This greeting of the Lord is a bridge that he builds between heaven and earth.

*Homily for Pentecost at St. Peter's Basilica*
*May 15, 2005*

### 13. The Eucharist

The Lord is always journeying to meet the world. … May our streets be streets of Jesus! May our houses be homes for him and with him! May our life of every day be penetrated by his presence. With this gesture, let us place under his eyes the sufferings of the sick, the solitude of young people and the elderly, temptations, fears – our entire life.

*Homily in the square before the*
*Basilica of St. John Lateran*
*May 26, 2005*

## 14. A vast and terrible desert

From a spiritual point of view, the world in which we find ourselves, often marked by unbridled consumerism, religious indifference and a secularism closed to transcendence, can appear a desert just as "vast and terrible" (*Dt* 8:15) as the one we heard about in the first reading from the Book of Deuteronomy.

*Homily at closing of the*
*24ᵗʰ Italian National Eucharistic Congress, Bari*
*May 29, 2005*

## 15. The path

The path God points out to us through his Word goes in the direction inscribed in man's very existence. The Word of God and reason go together. For the human being, following the Word of God, going with Christ means fulfilling oneself; losing it is equivalent to losing oneself.

*Homily at closing of the*
*24ᵗʰ Italian National Eucharistic Congress, Bari*
*May 29, 2005*

## 16. Forgiveness

We cannot communicate with the Lord if we do not communicate with one another. If we want to present ourselves to him, we must also take a step towards meeting one another. To do this we must learn the great lesson of forgiveness: we must not let the gnawing of resentment work in our soul, but must open our hearts to the magnanimity of listening to others, open our hearts to understanding them, eventually to accepting their apologies, to generously offering our own.

*Homily at closing of the*
*24ᵗʰ Italian National Eucharistic Congress, Bari*
*May 29, 2005*

## 17. To the youth

Young people must feel loved by the Church. … In this way they will experience in the Church the Lord's friendship and love for them and understand that in Christ, truth coincides with love. In turn, they will learn to love the Lord and to trust in his Body, which is the Church.

*Address to the 54th Assembly of Italian Bishops*
*May 30, 2005*

## JUNE 2005

### 18. With Christ's sentiments

Christ, incarnate and humiliated by the most shameful death of crucifixion, is held up as a vital model for Christians. Indeed ... their "attitude must be that of Christ" (cf. *Phil* 2:5), and their sentiments, humility and self-giving, detachment and generosity.

*Catechesis to the General Audience*
*June 1, 2005*

## 19. Religious education

The educational relationship is delicate by nature: in fact, it calls into question the freedom of the other who, however gently, is always led to make a decision. Neither parents nor priests nor catechists, nor any other educators can substitute for the freedom of the child, adolescent, or young person whom they are addressing. The proposal of Christianity in particular challenges the very essence of freedom and calls it to faith and conversion.

*Address to the Ecclesial Diocesan Convention of Rome*
*in the Basilica of St. John Lateran*
*June 6, 2005*

## 20. Jesus' sacrifice

The Church is not "holy" by herself; in fact, she is made up of sinners – we all know this and it is plain for all to see. Rather, she is made holy ever anew by the Holy One of God, by the purifying love of Christ. God did not only speak, but loved us very realistically; he loved us to the point of the death of his own Son.

*Homily at St. Peter's Basilica*
*June 29, 2005*

## JULY 2005

### 21. The way

For suffering itself is the way to transformation, and without suffering nothing is transformed.

*Address to the meeting with the diocesan clergy of Aosta*
*at the parish church at Introd (Aosta Valley)*
*July 25, 2005*

### 22. *Quasi Deus daretur*

There is no longer any proof of moral values. They become evident only if God exists. ... We must live *"quasi Deus daretur,"* and even if we are not strong enough to believe, we must live on this hypothesis, otherwise the world will not function.

*Address to the meeting with the diocesan clergy of Aosta*
*at the parish church at Introd (Aosta Valley)*
*July 25, 2005*

## 23. The inner life

It is necessary to understand that building life and the future also requires patience and suffering. Nor can the cross be lacking in young peoples' lives, and getting them to understand this is far from easy. The mountaineer knows that he must face sacrifices and train if climbing is to be a beautiful experience; so too, the young person must understand that for the ascent to life's future it is essential to exercise an interior life.

*Address to the meeting with the diocesan clergy of Aosta*
*at the parish church at Introd (Aosta Valley)*
*July 25, 2005*

## 24. Joy

Once again, it is necessary to make it clear that pleasure is not everything. May Christianity give us joy, just as love gives joy. But love is always also a renunciation of self. The Lord himself has given us the formula of what love is: those who lose themselves find themselves; those who spare or save themselves are lost. It is always an "Exodus," hence, painful. True joy is something different from pleasure; joy grows and continues to mature in suffering, in communion with the Cross of Christ. It is here alone that the true joy of faith is born.

*Address to the meeting with the diocesan clergy of Aosta*
*at the parish church at Introd (Aosta Valley)*
*July 25, 2005*

# AUGUST 2005

## 25. Worship

But what does "worship" mean? Might it be an expression of past times, meaningless to our contemporaries? No! … [It] is full of gratitude that wells up from the depths of their heart and floods their entire being, for it is only by adoring and loving God above all things that human beings can totally fulfill themselves.

*Angelus*
*August 7, 2005*

## 26. Wings

The widespread idea which continues to exist is that Christianity is composed of laws and bans which one has to keep and, hence, is something toilsome and burdensome – that one is freer without such a burden. I want to make it clear that it is not a burden to be carried by a great love and realization, but is like having wings. It is wonderful to be a Christian.

*Interview with Vatican Radio*
*August 14, 2005*

## 27. Wisdom

Wisdom in itself is not something stale … but it is the understanding of the facts of the matter, it is the view of what is "essential." … That is what the wisdom of belief is about, not that we know many details – that is important for every job – but, that we know, above all, the details of what life is about and how being human, and the future, is to be shaped.

*Interview with Vatican Radio*
*August 14, 2005*

## 28. Europe's Christian roots

I think that this civilization, with all its dangers and hopes, can only lead to greatness if it is tamed: if it recognizes her own springs of strength, if we again see the greatness, that give this endangered possibility of human existence a direction and greatness. If we're happy to be living on this continent which has determined the world's fate – for good and bad – and undertake the on-going task to rediscover the truth, purity, and greatness which gives us our future – we will continuously, and even in new and better ways, stand in the service of all humanity.

*Interview with Vatican Radio*
*August 14, 2005*

## 29. The crisis of modernity

Previously, it was thought and believed that by setting God aside and being autonomous, following only our own ideas and inclinations, we would truly be free to do whatever we liked without anyone being able to give us orders. But when God disappears, men and women do not become greater; indeed, they lose the divine dignity, their faces lose God's splendor. In the end, they turn out to be merely products of a blind evolution and, as such, can be used and abused. This is precisely what the experience of our epoch has confirmed for us. Only if God is great is humankind also great.

*Homily to parish church of Castel Gandolfo*
*August 15, 2005*

## 30. "Those who sow in tears will reap with cries of joy" (*Ps* 126:5)

Under the burden of work, their faces are sometimes lined with tears: the sowing is laborious, perhaps doomed to uselessness and failure. But with the coming of the abundant, joyful harvest, they discover that their suffering has borne fruit. The great lesson on the mystery of life's fruitfulness that suffering can contain is condensed in this Psalm.

*Catechesis to the General Audience*
*August 17, 2005*

## 31. Faithfulness

In the end, perseverance in good, even if it is misunderstood and opposed, always reaches a landing place of light, fruitfulness, and peace.

*Catechesis to the General Audience*
*August 17, 2005*

## 32. The star

The Magi set out because of a deep desire which prompted them to leave everything and begin a journey. It was as though they had always been waiting for that star. It was as if the journey had always been a part of their destiny, and was finally about to begin.

*Address to seminarians in Cologne, August 19, 2005*

## 33. A circle

The better you know Jesus the more his mystery attracts you. The more you discover him, the more you are moved to seek him.

*Address to seminarians in Cologne, August 19, 2005*

## 34. Holiness

The secret of holiness is friendship with Christ and faithful obedience to his will.

*Address to seminarians in Cologne, August 19, 2005*

## 35. The inner way

The new King, to whom they [the Magi] now paid homage, was quite unlike what they were expecting. In this way they had to learn that God is not as we usually imagine him to be. This was where their inner journey began. ... By serving and following him, they wanted, together with him, to serve the cause of good and the cause of justice in the world. In this they were right. Now, though, they have to learn that this cannot be achieved simply through issuing commands from a throne on high. Now they have to learn to give themselves – no lesser gift would be sufficient for this King. Now they have to learn that their lives must be conformed to this divine way of exercising power, to God's own way of being. They must become men of truth, of justice, of goodness, of forgiveness, of mercy. They will no longer ask: how can this serve me? Instead, they will have to ask: how can I serve God's presence in the world? They must learn to lose their life and in this way to find it.

*Address to the 20<sup>th</sup> World Youth Day*
*in Cologne – Marienfeld, August 20, 2005*

## 36. The gift of self

The saints and the blessed did not doggedly seek their own happiness, but simply wanted to give themselves, because the light of Christ had shone upon them. They show us the way to attain happiness; they show us how to be truly human.

*Address to the 20 th World Youth Day*
*in Cologne – Marienfeld*
*August 20, 2005*

## 37. Freedom

Freedom is not simply about enjoying life in total autonomy, but rather about living by the measure of truth and goodness, so that we ourselves can become true and good.

*Homily at the 20 th World Youth Day*
*in Cologne – Marienfeld*
*August 21, 2005*

## 38. Availability

If we think and live according to our communion with Christ, then our eyes will be opened. Then we will no longer be content to scrape a living just for ourselves, but we will see where and how we are needed. Living and acting thus, we will soon realize that it is much better to be useful and at the disposal of others than to be concerned only with the comforts that are offered to us.

*Homily at the 20ᵗʰ World Youth Day*
*in Cologne – Marienfeld*
*August 21, 2005*

### 39. Seeking and finding

Faith is not merely the attachment to a complex of dogmas, complete in itself, that is supposed to satisfy the thirst for God, present in the human heart. On the contrary, it guides human beings on their way through time toward a God who is ever new in his infinity. Christians, therefore, are at the same time both seekers and finders.

*Angelus*
*August 28, 2005*

### 40. Abandonment

In the serene and faithful abandonment of our freedom to the Lord, our work also becomes solid, capable of bearing lasting fruit. Thus, our "sleep" [cf. *Ps* 127:2] becomes rest blessed by God and destined to seal an activity that has meaning and coherence.

*Catechesis to the General Audience*
*August 31, 2005*

## SEPTEMBER 2005

### 41. The sign of the cross

Making the sign of the cross – as we will do during the blessing – means saying a visible and public "yes" to the One who died and rose for us, to God who in the humility and weakness of his love is the Almighty, stronger than all the power and intelligence of the world.

*Angelus*
*September 11, 2005*

## 42. The temple

At the heart of the social life of a city, of a community, of a people there must be a presence that calls to mind the mystery of the transcendent God, a proper space for God, a dwelling for God. Man cannot walk well without God; he must walk together with God through history, and the task of the temple, of the dwelling of God, is to point out in a visible way this communion.

*Catechesis to the General Audience*
*September 14, 2005*

### 43. *Dei Verbum*

The Church does not live on herself but on the Gospel, and in the Gospel always and ever anew finds the directions for her journey. This is a point that every Christian must understand and apply to himself or herself: only those who first listen to the Word can become preachers of it. Indeed, they must not teach their own wisdom but the wisdom of God, which often appears to be foolishness in the eyes of the world (cf. 1 *Cor* 1:23).

*Address to the International Congress on*
*the 40 th Anniversary of "Dei Verbum"*
*in Castel Gandolfo*
*September 16, 2005*

### 44. *Lex credendi*

Believing consists in entrusting ourselves to God, who knows and loves us personally, and in accepting the truth he has revealed in Christ with the confidence that leads us to trust in him, the Revealer of the Father. He loves us despite our shortcomings and sins and his love gives meaning to our lives and to the life of the world.

*Address to newly appointed bishops*
*in Castel Gandolfo, September 19, 2005*

### 45. The primacy of spiritual life

Answering God requires the believer to make that inner journey which leads him or her to an encounter with the Lord. The encounter is only possible if the person can open his or her heart to God, who speaks in the depths of the conscience. This requires interiority, silence, and watchfulness.

*Address to newly appointed bishops*
*in Castel Gandolfo, September 19, 2005*

## 46. Human commitment

Men and women must respond with faithful and active loyalty to God's promise and gift, which have nothing magical about them, in a dialogue in which are interwoven two freedoms, the divine and the human.

*Catechesis to the General Audience*
*September 21, 2005*

## 47. *Lex orandi*

The prayer of a priest is a requirement of his pastoral ministry. This is because no community can forego the witness of a prayerful priest who proclaims transcendence and is immersed in God's mystery.

*Address to Mexican bishops during their*
*ad limina visit to Castel Gandolfo*
*September 23, 2005*

## 48. The Kingdom of God

Confronted by today's changing and complex panorama, the virtue of hope is subject to harsh trials in the community of believers. For this very reason, we must be apostles who are filled with hope and joyful trust in God's promises. God never abandons his people; indeed, he invites them to conversion so that his Kingdom may become a reality. The Kingdom of God does not only mean that God exists, that he is alive, but also that he is present and active in the world. He is the most intimate and crucial reality in every act of human life, every moment of history.

*Address to Mexican bishops during their*
*ad limina visit to Castel Gandolfo*
*September 23, 2005*

## 49. Freedom

Many of them [young people] erroneously imagine that commitment and making definitive decisions entail the loss of freedom. It is right to remind them, instead, that people become free when they unconditionally commit themselves to truth and goodness. Only in this way, if they keep Jesus at the center of their lives, will they be able to give life meaning and build something important and lasting.

*Address to Mexican bishops during their*
*ad limina visit to Castel Gandolfo*
*September 29, 2005*

# OCTOBER 2006

## 50. Water and wine

Water makes the earth fertile: it is the fundamental gift that makes life possible. Wine, on the other hand, expresses the excellence of creation and gives us the feast in which we go beyond the limits of our daily routine: wine, the Psalm says, "gladdens the heart."

*Homily to the General Assembly of the*
*Synod of Bishops at the Vatican Basilica*
*October 2, 2005*

## 51. Hypocrisy

The tolerance that admits God as it were as a private opinion but refuses him the public domain, the reality of the world and of our lives, is not tolerance but hypocrisy.

*Homily to the General Assembly of the*
*Synod of Bishops at the Vatican Basilica*
*October 2, 2005*

## 52. Idolatry

An idol is merely "a work of human hands" [*Ps* 135:15], a product of human desires, hence, powerless to overcome the limitations of creatures. Indeed, it has a human form with a mouth, eyes, ears and throat, but it is inert, lifeless, like an inanimate statue. Those who worship these dead realities are destined to resemble them, impotent, fragile, and inert. This description of idolatry as false religion clearly conveys man's eternal temptation to seek salvation in the "work of his hands," placing hope in riches, power, in success and material things.

*Catechesis to the General Audience*
*October 5, 2005*

## 53. Theology and spirituality

Spirituality does not attenuate the scientific charge, but impresses upon theological study the right method for achieving a coherent interpretation.

*Message for the centenary of the
birth of Hans Urs Von Balthasar
October 6, 2005*

## 54. Testimony

Faith cannot be reduced to a private sentiment or indeed, be hidden when it is inconvenient; it also implies consistency and a witness even in the public arena for the sake of human beings, justice, and truth.

*Angelus
October 9, 2005*

## 55. Mission

The dismissal at the end of Mass: *"Ite, missa est,"* which recalls the *"missio,"* the task of those who have taken part in the celebration to bring to everyone the Good News they have received and with it, to bring life to society.

*Angelus*
*October 9, 2005*

## 56. Justice and faith

Religion is neither abstract nor intimistic, but a leaven of justice and solidarity. Communion with God is necessarily followed by the communion of brothers and sisters with one another.

*Catechesis to the General Audience*
*October 12, 2005*

## 57. The city of hope

We must be a true Jerusalem in the Church today, that is, a place of peace, "supporting one another" as we are; "supporting one another together" in the joyful certainty that the Lord "supports us all."

*Catechesis to the General Audience*
*October 12, 2005*

## 58. Invisible and essential

It is precisely the invisible things that are the most profound, the most important. So let us go to meet this invisible but powerful Lord who helps us to live well. We do not see an electric current, for example, yet we see that it exists; we see this microphone, that it is working, and we see lights. Therefore, we do not see the very deepest things, those that really sustain life and the world, but we can see and feel their effects. This is also true for electricity; we do not see the electric current but we see the light. So it is with the Risen Lord: we do not see him with our eyes but we see that wherever Jesus is, people change, they improve. A greater capacity for peace, for reconciliation, etc., is created. Therefore, we do not see the Lord himself but we see the effects of the Lord: so we can understand that Jesus is present.

*Catechetical meeting with children*
*who had received their First Communion*
*October 15, 2005*

### 59. The absence of God

If God is absent from my life, if Jesus is absent from my life, a guide, an essential friend is missing, even an important joy for life, the strength to grow as a man, to overcome my vices and mature as a human being.

*Catechetical meeting with children who had*
*received their First Communion*
*October 15, 2005*

### 60. Singing and flying

The image of the sparrow [cf. *Ps* 84:4] is a joyful one, through which the psalmist wants to say that his entire life has become a song. He can sing and fly. Singing itself is almost like flying, rising up to God; it is in some way an anticipation of eternity when we will be able to "unceasingly sing God's praise."

*Address at the end of the concert by the*
*Regensburg Cathedral Boys Choir in the Sistine Chapel,*
*October 22, 2005*

## 61. Holiness

The saint is the person who is so fascinated by the beauty of God and by his perfect truth as to be progressively transformed by it.

*Address at the conclusion of the Synod of Bishops*
*October 23, 2005*

## 62. The little things

Joy is often found behind little things and is reached by following one's proper daily duty with a spirit of devotion.

*Address to pilgrims in Rome for the canonization of*
*five new saints in the Paul VI Audience Hall*
*October 24, 2005*

### 63. Responsibility

"He, Jesus, loves us" (Gregory of Nazianzen, *Carmina arcana, 2: Collana di Testi Patristici,* LVIII, Rome, 1986, pp. 236-238). These tender words are a great consolation and comfort for us; but also a great responsibility, day after day.

*Catechesis to the General Audience*
*October 26, 2005*

### 64. Similar to Jesus

"Have this mind among yourselves, which was in Christ Jesus" (cf. *Phil* 2:5). To learn to feel as Jesus felt; to conform our way of thinking, deciding and acting to the sentiments of Jesus. We will take up this path if we look to conform our sentiments to those of Jesus. Let us take up the right path.

*Catechesis to the General Audience*
*October 26, 2005*

## NOVEMBER 2005

### 65. Happiness according to God

Happy is the man who gives; happy is the man who does not live life for himself but gives; happy is the man who is merciful, generous, and just; happy is the man who lives in the love of God and neighbor. In this way we live well and have no reason to fear death because we experience the everlasting happiness that comes from God.

*Catechesis to the General Audience*
*November 2, 2005*

## 66. Catechesis

Be under no illusion. An incomplete Catholic teaching is a contradiction in itself and cannot be fruitful in the long term. The proclamation of the Kingdom of God goes hand in hand with the need for conversion and love that encourages, that knows the way, that teaches an understanding that with God's grace even what seems impossible becomes possible.

*Address to Austrian bishops*
*on their ad limina visit*
*November 5, 2005*

## 67. God is demanding

God is not satisfied by the fact that his people pay him lip service. God wants their hearts and gives us his grace if we do not drift away or cut ourselves off from him.

*Address to Austrian bishops*
*on their ad limina visit*
*November 5, 2005*

### 68. Spiritual reading

"Spiritual reading" of Sacred Scripture consists in pouring over a biblical text for some time, reading it and rereading it, as it were, "ruminating" on it as the Fathers say and squeezing from it, so to speak, all its "juice," so that it may nourish meditation and contemplation and, like water, succeed in irrigating life itself.

*Angelus*
*November 6, 2005*

### 69. Testimony and words

The mission of the Church is to "witness" to the truth of Jesus Christ, the Word made flesh. Word and witness go together: the Word calls forth and gives form to the witness; the witness derives its authenticity from total fidelity to the Word.

*Address to the representative of the*
*Lutheran World Federation*
*November 7, 2005*

## 70. Atheism

Some people, "deceived by the atheism they bore within them, imagined that the universe lacked guidance and order, at the mercy as it were of chance" (Basil the Great, *Homilies on the Final Judgment*, 1, 2, 4). How many these "some people" are today! Deceived by atheism they consider and seek to prove that it is scientific to think that all things lack guidance and order as though they were at the mercy of chance. The Lord through Sacred Scripture reawakens our reason which has fallen asleep and tells us: in the beginning was the creative Word.

*Catechesis to the General Audience*
*November 9, 2005*

### 71. The way

Jesus is the way open to "all"; there are no others. And what seem to be "other" ways, lead to him if they are authentic, or else they do not lead to life.

*Homily Mass for*
*deceased cardinals and bishops of*
*the past year at the St. Peter's Basilica*
*November 11, 2005*

### 72. Trust in Christ

The Lord can always supplement any possible gaps and the meager means you have available. Rather than efficient organization, what counts is steadfast faith in Christ, for he also guides, governs, and sanctifies his Church through your indispensable ministry.

*Address to Bulgarian bishops*
*on their ad limina visit*
*November 12, 2005*

## 73. The risk

Our danger is that the memory of evil, of the evils suffered, may often be stronger than the memory of good. The Psalm's [cf. *Ps* 135] purpose is also to reawaken in us the memory of good as well as of all the good that the Lord has done and is doing for us, which we can perceive if we become deeply attentive. It is true, God's mercy endures for ever: it is present day after day.

*Catechesis to the General Audience*
*November 16, 2005*

## 74. The Christian community

The Christian community is a reality of people living by their own rules. It is a living body that, in Jesus, is in the world to bear witness to the power of the Gospel. It is, therefore, brothers and sisters who are gathered together without any aim of power or selfish interests, but who live in the joy the charity of God, who is love.

*Address to bishops from the Czech Republic*
*on their ad limina visit*
*November 18, 2005*

## 75. Limits to secularism

Believers, moreover, know well that the Gospel is in an intrinsic harmony with the values engraved in human nature. Thus, God's image is deeply impressed in the soul of the human being, the voice of whose conscience it is far from easy to silence.

*Address to the 20ᵗʰ International Conference on*
*the Human Genome*
*November 19, 2005*

## 76. The human person

Human beings are part of nature and, yet, as free subjects who have moral and spiritual values, they transcend nature. This anthropological reality is an integral part of Christian thought, and responds directly to the attempts to abolish the boundary between human sciences and natural sciences, often proposed in contemporary society.

*Address to the members of the*
*Pontifical Academy of Sciences*
*November 21, 2005*

## 77. The search of happiness

How easy it is to be content with the superficial pleasures that daily life offers us; how easy it is to live only for oneself, apparently enjoying life! But sooner or later we realize that this is not true happiness, because true happiness is much deeper: we find it only in Jesus.

*Message for the First National Day*
*of Young Catholics of the Netherlands*
*November 21, 2005*

## 78. True progress

Technical progress, necessary as it is, is not everything. True progress is that alone which integrally safeguards the dignity of the human being and which enables each people to share its own spiritual and material resources for the benefit of all.

*Address to the 33rd Conference of the United Nations*
*Food and Agriculture Organization (FAO)*
*November 24, 2005*

### 79. Faith and reason

The criterion of rationality, empirical proof by experimentation, has become ever more exclusive. The fundamental human questions – how to live and how to die – thus appear to be excluded from the context of rationality and are left to the sphere of subjectivity. ... This then is the great challenge ... : to impart knowledge in the perspective of true rationality, different from that of today which largely prevails, in accordance with a reason open to the question of the truth and to the great values inscribed in being itself, hence, open to the transcendent, to God.

*Address at the Catholic University of Rome*
*November 25, 2005*

## 80. Education in the faith (1)

We know that here it is not only a matter of didactics, of perfecting methods of transmitting knowledge, but also has to do with an education based on the direct, personal encounter with the person, on witness – that is, on the authentic transmission of faith, hope, and charity and the values that directly derive from these – from one person to another. Thus, it is an authentic meeting with another person who should first be listened to and understood.

*Address to bishops from Poland*
*on their ad limina visit*
*November 26, 2005*

## 81. Education in the faith (2)

Education in the faith must first of all consist in developing all that is good in the human being.

*Address to bishops from Poland*
*on their ad limina visit*
*November 26, 2005*

## 82. Through you

Are you willing to give me your flesh, your time, your life? This is the voice of the Lord who also wants to enter our epoch, he wants to enter human life through us. He also seeks a living dwelling place in our personal lives. This is the coming of the Lord. Let us once again learn this in the season of Advent: the Lord can also come among us.

*Homily at St. Peter's Basilica*
*November 26, 2005*

### 83. *Super flumina Babylonis*

[St. Augustine] knows that there are also people among the inhabitants of Babylon who are committed to peace and to the good of the community, although they do not share the biblical faith; the hope of the Eternal City to which we aspire is unknown to them. Within them they have a spark of desire for the unknown, for the greater, for the transcendent: for true redemption [cf. *Exposition on the Psalms,* 136, 1-2]. ... With this faith, even in an unknown reality, they are truly on their way towards the true Jerusalem, towards Christ. And with this openness of hope, Augustine also warns the "Babylonians," – as he calls them – those who do not know Christ or even God and yet desire the unknown, the eternal, and he warns us too, not to focus merely on the material things of the present but to persevere on the journey to God (*Ps* 167:1).

*Catechesis to the General Audience*
*November 30, 2005*

# DECEMBER 2005

## 84. Theology and contemplation

Theological work has meaning; it certainly requires scientific competence but likewise, and no less, the spirit of faith and the humility of those who know that God is alive and true, the subject of their reflection, who infinitely exceeds human capacities. Only with prayer and contemplation is it possible to acquire the sense of God and the docility to the Holy Spirit's action.

*Address to members of the*
*International Theological Commission*
*December 1, 2005*

## 85. Assent

As God is sovereignly free in revealing and giving himself because he is motivated solely by love, so the human person is also free in giving his or her own, even dutiful, assent: God expects a response of love.

*Angelus*
*December 4, 2005*

## 86. *Never forsake the work of your hands!*

We must be sure that however burdensome and tempestuous the trials that await us may be, we will never be left on our own, we will never fall out of the Lord's hands, those hands that created us and now sustain us on our journey through life (*Ps* 138:8).

*Catechesis to the General Audience*
*December 7, 2005*

## 87. Giving and finding oneself

The more the human person gives himself, the more he finds himself.

*Homily for the Solemnity of the*
*Immaculate Conception of the Blessed Virgin Mary*
*December 8, 2005*

## 88. Love

Love is not dependence but a gift that makes us live.

*Homily for the Solemnity of the*
*Immaculate Conception of the Blessed Virgin Mary*
*December 8, 2005*

## 89. Communion of freedom

The freedom of a human being is the freedom of a limited being, and therefore is itself limited. We can possess it only as a shared freedom, in the communion of freedom: only if we live in the right way, with one another and for one another, can freedom develop.

*Homily for the Solemnity of the*
*Immaculate Conception of the Blessed Virgin Mary*
*December 8, 2005*

## 90. Closeness

The closer a person is to God, the closer he is to people.

*Homily for the Solemnity of the*
*Immaculate Conception of the Blessed Virgin Mary*
*December 8, 2005*

## 91. Courage!

Have the courage to dare with God! Try it! Do not be afraid of him! Have the courage to risk with faith! Have the courage to risk with goodness! Have the courage to risk with a pure heart! Commit yourselves to God, then you will see that it is precisely by doing so that your life will become broad and light, not boring but filled with infinite surprises, for God's infinite goodness is never depleted!

*Homily for the Solemnity of the*
*Immaculate Conception of the Blessed Virgin Mary*
*December 8, 2005*

## 92. Consecrated life

In the face of the advance of hedonism, the courageous witness of chastity is asked of you as the expression of a heart that knows the beauty and price of God's love. In the face of the thirst for money that widely prevails today, your sober life, ready to serve the neediest, is a reminder that God is the true treasure that does not perish. Before the individualism and relativism that induce people to be a rule unto themselves, your fraternal life, which can be coordinated and is thus capable of obedience, confirms that you place your fulfillment in God.

*Address to the men and women religious, members of*
*Secular Institutes and Societies of Apostolic Life*
*of the Rome Diocese*
*December 10, 2005*

### 93. Sustain

The gaze and the manifestation of the Lord of being and time even penetrates the darkness, in which it is difficult to move about and see. His hand is always ready to grasp ours, to lead us on our earthly journey (cf. *Ps* 139:10). This is not, therefore, a judgmental closeness that inspires terror, but a closeness of support and liberation.

*Catechesis to the General Audience*
*December 14, 2005*

### 94. The vocation of human beings

Believing in Christ means letting oneself be enveloped by the light of his truth, which gives full significance, value, and meaning to our lives, for precisely by revealing to us the mystery of the Father and his love for man, he also fully reveals man to himself and brings to light his most high calling.

*Address to pilgrims from Upper Austria*
*at the Vatican's Hall of Blessing*
*December 17, 2005*

## 95. A child

God is not remote from us, unknown, enigmatic or perhaps dangerous. God is close to us, so close that he makes himself a child and we can informally address this God.

*Homily for the Fourth Sunday of Advent*
*December 18, 2005*

## 96. Joy

Joy is the true gift of Christmas, not expensive presents that demand time and money. We can transmit this joy simply: with a smile, with a kind gesture, with some small help, with forgiveness. Let us give this joy and the joy given will be returned to us.

*Homily for the Fourth Sunday of Advent*
*December 18, 2005*

## 97. The hands of God

This world of ours is a world of fear: the fear of misery and poverty, the fear of illness and suffering, the fear of solitude, the fear of death. We have in this world a widely developed insurance system; it is good that it exists. But we know that at the moment of deep suffering, at the moment of the ultimate loneliness of death, no insurance policy will be able to protect us. The only valid insurance in those moments is the one that comes to us from the Lord, who also assures us: "Do not fear, I am always with you." We can fall, but in the end we fall into God's hands, and God's hands are good hands.

*Homily for the Fourth Sunday of Advent*
*December 18, 2005*

## 98. Joseph's silence

The silence of St. Joseph is given a special emphasis. His silence is steeped in contemplation of the mystery of God in an attitude of total availability to the divine desires. It is a silence thanks to which Joseph, in unison with Mary, watches over the Word of God, known through the Sacred Scriptures, continuously comparing it with the events of the life of Jesus; a silence woven of constant prayer, a prayer of blessing of the Lord, of the adoration of his holy will and of unreserved entrustment to his providence. It is no exaggeration to think that it was precisely from his "father" Joseph that Jesus learned – at the human level – that steadfast interiority which is a presupposition of authentic justice. ... Let us allow ourselves to be "filled" with St. Joseph's silence! In a world that is often too noisy, that encourages neither recollection nor listening to God's voice.

*Angelus*
*December 18, 2005*

## 99. Brothers and sisters of Jesus

In the Child of Bethlehem, the smallness of God-made-man shows us the greatness of man and the beauty of our dignity as children of God and brothers and sisters of Jesus.

*Address to the members of the Catholic Action*
*December 19, 2005*

## 100. Spiritual light

As we look at the streets and squares of the cities decorated with dazzling lights, that these lights refer us to another light, invisible to the eyes but not to the heart. While we admire them, while we light the candles in churches or the illuminations of the crib and the Christmas tree in our homes, may our souls be open to the true spiritual light brought to all people of good will.

*Catechesis to the General Audience*
*December 21, 2005*

## 101. Meaning of suffering

We must do all we can to alleviate suffering and prevent the injustice that causes the suffering of the innocent. However, we must also do the utmost to ensure that people can discover the meaning of suffering and are thus able to accept their own suffering and to unite it with the suffering of Christ. In this way, it is merged with redemptive love and consequently becomes a force against the evil in the world.

*Address to the Roman Curia, December 22, 2005*

## 102. The Creator's handwriting

Not to see the world that surrounds us solely as raw material with which we can do something, but to try to discover in it "the Creator's handwriting," the creative reason and the love from which the world was born and of which the universe speaks to us, if we pay attention, if our inner senses awaken and acquire perception of the deepest dimensions of reality.

*Address to the Roman Curia, December 22, 2005*

## 103. Encounter and adoration

The Eucharist is the encounter and unification of persons; the person, however, who comes to meet us and desires to unite himself to us is the Son of God. Such unification can only be brought about by means of adoration. Receiving the Eucharist means adoring the One whom we receive. Precisely in this way and only in this way do we become one with him.

*Address to the Roman Curia*
*December 22, 2005*

## 104. April 19, 2005

Lastly, should I perhaps recall once again that April 19 this year on which, to my great surprise, the College of Cardinals elected me as the Successor of Pope John Paul II, as a Successor of St. Peter on the chair of the Bishop of Rome? Such an office was far beyond anything I could ever have imagined as my vocation. It was, therefore, only with a great act of trust in God that I was able to say in obedience my "yes" to this choice.

*Address to the Roman Curia*
*December 22, 2005*

### 105. *When I was being made …*
*Your eyes foresaw my actions*

Once again the transcendent greatness of divine knowledge emerges, embracing not only humanity's past and present but also the span, still hidden, of the future. However, the greatness of this little unborn human creature, formed by God's hands and surrounded by his love, also appears: a biblical tribute to the human being from the first moment of his existence (*Ps* 139:6).

*Catechesis to the General Audience*
*December 28, 2005*

### 106. Taking care of God

God is like that: he does not impose himself, he never uses force to enter, but asks, as a child does, to be welcomed. In a certain sense, God too presents himself in need of attention: he waits for us to open our hearts to him, to take care of him.

*Address to the "St. Martha's" dispensary*
*in Vatican City, December 30, 2005*

# JANUARY 2006

## 107. In truth, peace

When man allows himself to be enlightened by the splendor of truth, he inwardly becomes a courageous peacemaker.

*Angelus*
*January 1, 2006*

## 108. Peace is not the lack of war

We need to regain an awareness that we share a common destiny which is ultimately transcendent, so as to maximize our historical and cultural differences, not in opposition to, but in cooperation with, people belonging to other cultures. These simple truths are what make peace possible; they are easily understood whenever we listen to our own hearts with pure intentions. Peace thus comes to be seen in a new light: not as the mere absence of war, but as a harmonious coexistence of individual citizens within a society governed by justice, one in which the good is also achieved, to the extent possible, for each of them.

*Message for the celebration of the World Day of Peace, January 1, 2006*

## 109. The true progress

Yes, there is progress in history. There is, we could say, an evolution of history. Progress is all that which brings us closer to Christ and thus closer to a united humanity, to true humanism. And so, hidden within these indications there is also an imperative for us: to work for progress, something that we all want. We can do this by working to bring others to Christ; we can do this by personally conforming ourselves to Christ, thereby taking up the path of true progress.

*Catechesis to the General Audience*
*January 4, 2006*

## 110. The Christian paradox

In the Child of Bethlehem, God revealed himself in the humility of the "human form," in the "form of a slave," indeed, of one who died on a cross (cf. *Phil* 2:6-8). This is the Christian paradox. Indeed, this very concealment constitutes the most eloquent "manifestation" of God. The humility, poverty, even the ignominy of the Passion enable us to know what God is truly like.

*Homily at the Vatican Basilica, January 6, 2006*

## 111. God's family

No one of us knows what will happen on our planet, on our European Continent, in the next fifty, sixty, or seventy years. But we can be sure of one thing: God's family will always be present and those who belong to this family will never be alone. They will always be able to fall back on the steadfast friendship of the One who is life.

*Homily in the Sistine Chapel, January 8, 2006*

## 112. The cross

The cross sums up Jesus' life.

*Homily in the Sistine Chapel, January 8, 2006*

## 113. Truth and life

The truths of the spirit, the truths about good and evil, about the great goals and horizons of life, about our relationship with God. These truths cannot be attained without profound consequences for the way we live our lives.

*Address to the Diplomatic Corps to the Holy See*
*January 9, 2006*

## 114. Truth and freedom

The right to freedom of religion, since it involves the most important of human relationships: our relationship with God. To all those responsible for the life of nations I wish to state: if you do not fear truth, you need not fear freedom!

*Address to the Diplomatic Corps to the Holy See*
*January 9, 2006*

## 115. Knowledge of God

It is important in our time that we do not forget God, together with all the other kinds of knowledge we have acquired in the meantime, and they are very numerous! They all become problematic, at times dangerous, if the fundamental knowledge that gives meaning and orientation to all things is missing: knowledge of God the Creator.

*Catechesis to the General Audience*
*January 11, 2006*

## 116. Dark nights

To be a disciple of Christ: for a Christian this suffices. Friendship with the Teacher guarantees profound peace and serenity to the soul even in the dark moments and in the most arduous trials. When faith meets with dark nights, in which the presence of God is no longer "felt" or "seen," friendship with Jesus guarantees that in reality nothing can ever separate us from his love.

*Angelus, January 15, 2006*

## 117. A fundamental option

Faith is not a theory that can be personalized or even set aside. It is something very concrete: it is the criterion that determines our lifestyle.

*Address to the Pontifical Council "Cor Unum"*
*January 23, 2006*

## 118. To know God

Only a people that knows God and defends spiritual and moral values can truly go towards a profound peace and also become a strength of peace for the world and for others.

*Catechesis to the General Audience*
*January 25, 2006*

### 119. *Mysterium communionis*

True love does not eliminate legitimate differences, but harmonizes them in a superior unity that is not ordered from the "outside" but gives form from "within," so to speak, to the whole. It is the mystery of communion.

*Homily during vespers on the Feast of the*
*Conversion of St. Paul at the conclusion of the*
*Week of Prayer for Christian Unity*
*January 25, 2006*

### 120. The fundamentals of love

"We have come to believe in God's love" [cf. 1 *Jn* 4:16]: in these words the Christian can express the fundamental decision of his life. Being Christian is not the result of an ethical choice or a lofty idea, but the encounter with an event, a person, which gives life a new horizon and a decisive direction.

*Encyclical Letter* Deus Caritas Est, *no. 1*
*(published January 25, 2006)*

### 121. Eros and agape

Love is indeed "ecstasy," not in the sense of a moment of intoxication, but rather as a journey, an ongoing exodus out of the closed inward-looking self towards its liberation through self-giving, and thus towards authentic self-discovery and indeed the discovery of God.

*Encyclical Letter* Deus Caritas Est, *no. 6*

### 122. Unprecedented realism

The real novelty of the New Testament lies not so much in new ideas as in the figure of Christ himself, who gives flesh and blood to those concepts – an unprecedented realism.

*Encyclical Letter* Deus Caritas Est, *no. 12*

### 123. The commandment of love

Love can be "commanded" because it has first been given (cf. *Mk* 12:31).

*Encyclical Letter* Deus Caritas Est, *no. 14*

### 124. The gaze of Jesus

Seeing with the eyes of Christ, I can give to others much more than their outward necessities; I can give them the look of love that they crave.

*Encyclical Letter* Deus Caritas Est, *no. 18*

### 125. "By chance"

The parable of the Good Samaritan remains as a standard which imposes universal love towards the needy whom we encounter "by chance" (cf. *Lk* 10:31), whoever they may be.

*Encyclical Letter* Deus Caritas Est, *no. 25b*

### 126. Christian humanism

We all have the same fundamental motivation and look towards the same goal: a true humanism, which acknowledges that man is made in the image of God and wants to help him to live in a way consonant with that dignity.

*Encyclical Letter* Deus Caritas Est, *no. 30b*

## 127. Speaking and saying nothing

[Who practice charity] realize that a pure and generous love is the best witness to the God in whom we believe and by whom we are driven to love. A Christian knows when it is time to speak of God and when it is better to say nothing and to let love alone speak. He knows that God is love (cf. 1 *Jn* 4:8) and that God's presence is felt at the very time when the only thing we do is to love.

*Encyclical Letter* Deus Caritas Est, *no. 31c*

## 128. Urgency of prayer

People who pray are not wasting their time, even though the situation appears desperate and seems to call for action alone.

*Encyclical Letter* Deus Caritas Est, *no. 36*

### 129. God's incomprehensibility

Certainly Job could complain before God about the presence of incomprehensible and apparently unjustified suffering in the world [cf. *Jb* 23:3, 5-6, 15-16]. … Often we cannot understand why God refrains from intervening. Yet he does not prevent us from crying out, like Jesus on the Cross: "My God, my God, why have you forsaken me?" (*Mt* 27:46). We should continue asking this question in prayerful dialogue before his face: "Lord, holy and true, how long will it be?" (*Rv* 6:10). It is St. Augustine who gives us faith's answer to our sufferings: *"Si comprehendis, non est Deus"* – "If you understand him, he is not God" (Sermon 52, 16; PL 38, 360).

*Encyclical Letter* Deus Caritas Est, *no. 38*

### 130. Hope

Faith, hope and charity go together. Hope is practiced through the virtue of patience, which continues to do good even in the face of apparent failure, and through the virtue of humility, which accepts God's mystery and trusts him even at times of darkness.

*Encyclical Letter* Deus Caritas Est, *no. 39*

### 131. *Magnificat anima mea dominum*

"My soul magnifies the Lord" (*Lk* 1:46). In these words she [Mary] expresses her whole program of life: not setting herself at the center, but leaving space for God, who is encountered both in prayer and in service of neighbor – only then does goodness enter the world. Mary's greatness consists in the fact that she wants to magnify God, not herself.

*Encyclical Letter* Deus Caritas Est, *no. 41*

# FEBRUARY 2006

## 132. The sword of pain

Mary thus shows that her role in the history of salvation did not end in the mystery of the Incarnation but was completed in loving and sorrowful participation in the death and Resurrection of her Son.

*Homily on the Feast of the Presentation of the Lord*
*at the Vatican Basilica*
*February 2, 2006*

## 133. The primacy of God

Whenever God is not there, the human being is no longer respected either. Only if God's splendor shines on the human face, is the human image of God protected by a dignity, which subsequently no one must violate.

*Homily in the Parish of St. Anna*
*February 5, 2006*

## 134. Cultivating and protecting

Man is not the master of life; rather, he is its custodian and steward.

*Homily in the Parish of St. Anna*
*February 5, 2006*

## 135. Respecting life

The word "respect" derives from the Latin word *respicere,* to look at, and means a way of looking at things and people that leads to recognizing their substantial character, not to appropriate them but rather to treat them with respect and to take care of them. In the final analysis, if creatures are deprived of their reference to God as a transcendent basis, they risk being at the mercy of the will of man who, as we see, can make an improper use of it.

*Homily in the Parish of St. Anna*
*February 5, 2006*

### 136. Contemporary hedonism

In the so-called society of well-being, life is exalted as long as it is pleasurable, but there is a tendency to no longer respect it as soon as it is sick or handicapped. Based on deep love for every person it is possible instead to put into practice effective forms of service to life: to new-born life and to life marked by marginalization or suffering, especially in its terminal phase.

*Angelus, February 5, 2006*

### 137. Contact

In our difficulties, problems, temptations, we must not simply make a theoretical reflection – where do they come from? – but must react positively; we must call on the Lord, we must keep alive our contact with the Lord. Indeed, we must cry out the Name of Jesus: "Jesus, help me!" And let us be certain that he hears us, because he is close to those who seek him [cf. *Ps* 145:18].

*Catechesis to the General Audience, February 8, 2006*

## 138. Truth, liberty, charity

The light that shines out from Jesus is the splendor of the truth. Every other truth is a fragment of the Truth that he is, and refers to him. Jesus is the Pole Star of human freedom: without him it loses its sense of direction, for without the knowledge of the truth, freedom degenerates, becomes isolated and is reduced to sterile arbitration. With him, freedom is rediscovered, it is recognized to have been created for our good and is expressed in charitable actions and behavior.

*Address to the Congregation for the Doctrine of the Faith*
*February 10, 2006*

## 139. Searching

Nothing succeeds as well as love for the truth in impelling the human mind towards unexplored horizons.

*Address to the Congregation for the Doctrine of the Faith*
*February 10, 2006*

### 140. Every trial

Every trial accepted with resignation is meritorious and draws divine goodness upon the whole of humanity.

*Message for the 14<sup>th</sup> World Day of the Sick*
*February 11, 2006*

### 141. All one

Jesus stood before man in his wholeness in order to heal him completely, in body, mind, and spirit. Indeed, the human person is a unity and his various dimensions can and must be distinguished but not separated.

*Address to the sick at the end of Mass*
*February 11, 2006*

## 142. Christ the doctor

Illness is a typical feature of the human condition, to the point that it can become a realistic metaphor of it, as St. Augustine expresses clearly in his prayer: "Have mercy on me, Lord! See: I do not hide my wounds from you. You are the doctor, I am the sick person; you are merciful, I am wretched" (Conf. X, 39).

*Angelus*
*February 12, 2006*

## 143. Generating Christ

The Lord can find a dwelling place in our own souls and lives. Not only must we carry him in our hearts, but also we must bring him to the world, so that we too can bring forth Christ for our epoch.

*Catechesis to the General Audience*
*February 15, 2006*

## 144. Signs of the times

Today, in fact, a culture marked by individual-istic relativism and positivist scientism is contin-uing to gain ground. It is a culture, therefore, that is tendentially closed to God and to his moral law, even if not always prejudicially opposed to Christianity. A great effort is there-fore asked of Catholics to increase dialogue with the contemporary culture in order to open it to the perennial values of transcendence.

*Address to the writers of* La Civiltà Cattolica
*February 17, 2006*

### 145. The light of the word

Dear young people. ... On life's journey, which is neither easy nor free of deceptions, you will meet difficulties and suffering and at times you will be tempted to exclaim with the psalmist: "I am severely afflicted" (*Ps* 119:107). Do not forget to add as the psalmist did: "give me life, O Lord, according to your word" *(ibid.)*. The loving presence of God, through his word, is the lamp that dispels the darkness of fear and lights up the path even when times are most difficult (cf. *Ps* 119:15).

> *Message to the youth of the 21ˢᵗ World Youth Day*
> *February 22, 2006*

### 146. An understanding heart

The secret of acquiring "an understanding heart" is to train your heart to "listen."

> *Message to the youth of the 21ˢᵗ World Youth Day*
> *February 22, 2006*

## 147. Mercy

Love must not simply abide by earthly laws but must let itself be illumined by the truth which is God and must be expressed in that superior measure of justice which is mercy.

*Address to the bishops from Bosnia and Herzegovina*
*on their ad limina visit*
*February 24, 2006*

## 148. The shadow of the father

The example of St. Joseph, a "just man," the Evangelist says, fully responsible before God and before Mary, should be an encouragement to all of you on your way towards the priesthood. Joseph appears to us ever attentive to the voice of the Lord, who guides the events of history, and ready to follow the instructions, ever faithful, generous and detached in service, an effective teacher of prayer and of work in the hidden life at Nazareth. I can assure you, dear seminarians, that the further you advance with God's grace on the path of the priesthood, the more you will experience what abundant spiritual fruits result from calling on St. Joseph and invoking his support in carrying out your daily duty.

*Address to the Roman Major Seminary*
*February 25, 2006*

## 149. The season of Lent

The season of Lent should not be faced with an "old" spirit, as if it were a heavy and tedious obligation, but with the new spirit of those who have found the meaning of life in Jesus and in his Paschal mystery and realize that henceforth everything must refer to him.

*Angelus*
*February 26, 2006*

### 150. Move forward

We have made enormous headway in our knowledge and have defined more clearly the limits of our ignorance but it always seems too arduous for human intelligence to realize that in looking at creation, we encounter the impression of the Creator. In fact, those who love the truth, like you, dear scholars, should perceive that research on such profound topics places us in the condition of seeing and, as it were, touching the hand of God. Beyond the limits of experimental methods ... wherever the perception of the senses no longer suffices or where neither the perception of the senses alone nor scientific verification is possible, begins the adventure of transcendence, the commitment to "go beyond" them.

*Address at the International Congress on the Human Embryo*
*February 27, 2006*

### 151. Integral charity

Who does not give God gives too little.

*Message for Lent 2006*

## MARCH 2006

### 152. Being rooted in the word

In the trials of life and in every temptation, the secret of victory lies in listening to the Word of truth and rejecting with determination falsehood and evil. This is the true and central program of the Lenten Season: to listen anew to the Gospel, the Word of the Lord, the word of truth, so that in every Christian, in every one of us, the understanding of the truth given to him, given to us, may be strengthened, so that we may live it and witness to it.

*Catechesis to the General Audience*
*March 1, 2006*

## 153. Followers of Christ

The response of those who follow Christ is rather to take the path chosen by the One who, in the face of the evils of his time and of all times, embraced the cross with determination, following the longer but more effective path of love.

*Homily for Ash Wednesday*
*March 1, 2006*

## 154. Choosing life

It is not by arrogating life to ourselves but only by giving life, not by having life and holding on to it but by giving it, that we can find it. This is the ultimate meaning of the cross: not to seek life for oneself, but to give one's own life.

*Address to the Roman Clergy*
*March 2, 2006*

## 155. Choosing God

Human life is a relationship. It is only in a relationship, and not closed in on ourselves, that we can have life. And the fundamental relationship is the relationship with the Creator, or else other relations are fragile. Hence, it is essential to choose God. A world empty of God, a world that has forgotten God, loses life and relapses into a culture of death.

*Address to the Roman Clergy*
*March 2, 2006*

## 156. To all mothers

One must thank mothers above all because they have had the courage to give life. And we must ask mothers to complete their gift by giving friendship with Jesus.

*Address to the Roman Clergy*
*March 2, 2006*

## 157. Openness

Faith, ultimately, is a gift. Consequently, the first condition is to let ourselves be given something, not to be self-sufficient or do everything by ourselves – because we cannot – but to open ourselves in the awareness that the Lord truly gives.

*Address to the Roman Clergy*
*March 2, 2006*

## 158. Communion of faith

No one believes purely on his own. We always believe in and with the Church. The Creed is always a shared act, it means letting ourselves be incorporated into a communion of progress, life, words, and thought. We do not "have" faith, in the sense that it is primarily God who gives it to us. Nor do we "have" it either, in the sense that it must not be invented by us. We must let ourselves fall, so to speak, into the communion of faith, of the Church.

*Address to the Roman Clergy*
*March 2, 2006*

## 159. Loneliness and incomprehension

The great problem of this time – in which each person, desiring to have life for himself, loses it because he is isolated and isolates the other from him – is to rediscover the deep communion which in the end can only stem from a foundation that is common to all souls, from the divine presence that unites all of us. I think that the condition for this is to overcome loneliness and misunderstanding, because the latter also results from the fact that thought today is fragmented. Each one seeks his own way of thinking and living and there is no communication in a profound vision of life.

*Address to the Roman Clergy*
*March 2, 2006*

## 160. Separate worlds

Young people feel exposed to new horizons which previous generations do not share; therefore, continuity in the vision of the world is absent, caught up as it is in an ever more rapid succession of new inventions. In ten years changes have taken place which previously never occurred in a hundred years. In this way worlds are really separated. ... We see that the world is changing at an ever faster pace, so that also with these changes it is fragmented. Therefore, at a moment of renewal and change, the element of stability becomes even more important.

*Address to the Roman Clergy*
*March 2, 2006*

## 161. Imperfections

Humility in accepting our own limitations is also very important. Only in this way, on the other hand, can we also grow, develop and pray to the Lord that he will help us not to tire along the way, also accepting humbly that we will never be perfect and accepting imperfections, especially in others. By accepting our own imperfections we can more easily accept those of others, allowing ourselves to be formed and reformed ever anew by the Lord.

*Address to the Roman Clergy*
*March 2, 2006*

## 162. Ecumenism

So this is very important: we must tolerate the separation that exists. St. Paul says that divisions are necessary for a certain time and that the Lord knows why: to test us, to train us, to develop us, to make us more humble. But at the same time, we are obliged to move towards unity, and moving towards unity is already a form of unity.

*Address to the Roman Clergy*
*March 2, 2006*

## 163. *Choosing life*

"Take up your cross and follow Christ" [cf. *Lk* 9:23], which means it is not necessary to seek your own life but to give life, and this is one interpretation of what "choosing life" means (*Dt* 30:19).

*Address to the Roman Clergy*
*March 2, 2006*

### 164. Temptations

To live life to the full in freedom we must overcome the test that this freedom entails, that is, temptation. Only if he is freed from the slavery of falsehood and sin can the human person, through the obedience of faith that opens him to the truth, find the full meaning of his life and attain peace, love, and joy.

*Angelus*
*March 5, 2006*

### 165. *Sacramentum exercitii*

We cannot bring to the world the Good News which is Christ himself in person, if we ourselves are not deeply united with Christ, if we do not know him profoundly, personally, if we do not live on his Words.

*Address at the close of the papal spiritual exercises*
*March 11, 2006*

### 166. Dwelling in the word

[Mary] lives her whole life in the Word of God. It is as though she were steeped in the Word. Thus, all her thoughts, her will, and her actions are imbued with and formed by the Word. Since she herself dwells in the Word, she can also become the new "Dwelling Place" of the Word in the world.

*Address at the close of the papal spiritual exercises*
*March 11, 2006*

### 167. With closed eyes

Human existence is a journey of faith and as such, moves ahead more in shadows than in full light, and is no stranger to moments of obscurity and also of complete darkness. While we are on this earth, our relationship with God takes place more by listening than by seeing; and the same contemplation comes about, so to speak, with closed eyes, thanks to the interior light that is kindled in us by the Word of God.

*Angelus, March 12, 2006*

## 168. Jesus and the Church

Between Christ and the Church there is no opposition. … Therefore, a slogan that was popular some years back: "Jesus yes, Church no," is totally inconceivable with the intention of Christ. … Between the Son of God-made-flesh and his Church there is a profound, unbreakable, and mysterious continuity by which Christ is present today in his people … and alive in the succession of the Apostles.

*Catechesis to the General Audience, March 15, 2006*

## 169. The Decalogue

The Commandments are the means that the Lord gives us to protect our freedom, both from the internal conditioning of passions and from the external abuse of those with evil intentions. The "nos" of the Commandments are as many "yeses" to the growth of true freedom.

*Homily on the Feast of St. Joseph*
*March 19, 2006*

## 170. The commandment of resting

It is indispensable that people not allow themselves to be enslaved by work or idolize it, claiming to find in it the ultimate and definitive meaning of life. ... The Sabbath is a holy day [*Ex* 20:8-9], that is, a day consecrated to God on which man understands better the meaning of his life and his work. It can therefore be said that the biblical teaching on work is crowned by the commandment of rest.

*Homily on the Feast of St. Joseph*
*March 19, 2006*

### 171. *Come and you shall see*

Come, so that you will be able to see [cf. *Jn* 1:38]. This is how the Apostles' adventure began, as an encounter of people who are open to one another. For the disciples, it was the beginning of a direct acquaintance with the Teacher, seeing where he was staying and starting to get to know him. Indeed, they were not to proclaim an idea, but to witness to a person. Before being sent out to preach, they had to "be" with Jesus (cf. *Mk* 3:14), establishing a personal relationship with him. On this basis, evangelization was to be no more than the proclamation of what they felt and an invitation to enter into the mystery of communion with Christ (cf. 1 *Jn* 1:3).

*Catechesis to the General Audience*
*March 22, 2006*

## 172. The annunciation

"Full of grace – *gratia plena*," which in the original Greek is *kecharitōménē*, "beloved" of God (cf. *Lk* 1:28) is a title expressed in passive form, but this "passivity" of Mary, who has always been and is forever "loved" by the Lord, implies her free consent, her personal and original response: in being loved, in receiving the gift of God, Mary is fully active, because she accepts with personal generosity the wave of God's love poured out upon her. In this too, she is the perfect disciple of her Son, who realizes the fullness of his freedom and thus exercises the freedom through obedience to the Father.

*Homily for the Concelebration*
*with the new Cardinals*
*March 25, 2006*

## 173. The cross

The cross … is the definitive "sign" par excellence given to us so that we might understand the truth about man and the truth about God: we have all been created and redeemed by a God who sacrificed his only Son out of love. This is why the Crucifixion … "is the culmination of that turning of God against himself in which he gives himself in order to raise man up and save him. This is love in its most radical form" (*Deus Caritas Est*, no. 12).

*Homily at the Roman parish of*
*Dio Padre Misericordioso*
*March 26, 2006*

## 174. *Koinonía*

Communion is also a gift with very real consequences. It lifts us from our loneliness, from being closed in on ourselves, and makes us sharers in the love that unites us to God and to one another. It is easy to understand how great this gift is if we only think of the fragmentation and conflicts that afflict relations between individuals, groups and entire peoples. … "Communion" is truly the Good News, the remedy given to us by the Lord to fight the loneliness that threatens everyone today, the precious gift that makes us feel welcomed and beloved by God, in the unity of his People gathered in the name of the Trinity.

*Catechesis to the General Audience*
*March 29, 2006*

## 175. Reconciliation

In order to respond to the call of God and start on our journey, it is not necessary to be already perfect. We know that the prodigal son's awareness of his own sin allowed him to set out on his return journey and thus feel the joy of reconciliation with the Father. Weaknesses and human limitations do not present an obstacle, as long as they help make us more aware of the fact that we are in need of the redeeming grace of Christ.

*Message for the*
*43rd World Day of Prayers for Vocations*
*March 30, 2006*

# INDEX

(Numbering refers to the
sequential positioning of each thought.)